Punk Coloring Book
by Gary Ellis
62 pages
noburbs press
3320 18th Street
San Francisco, CA 94110

Please use coloring materials that are suitable for the quality of the paper and printing of this publication.

ISBN 978-1717401052

printed in the USA

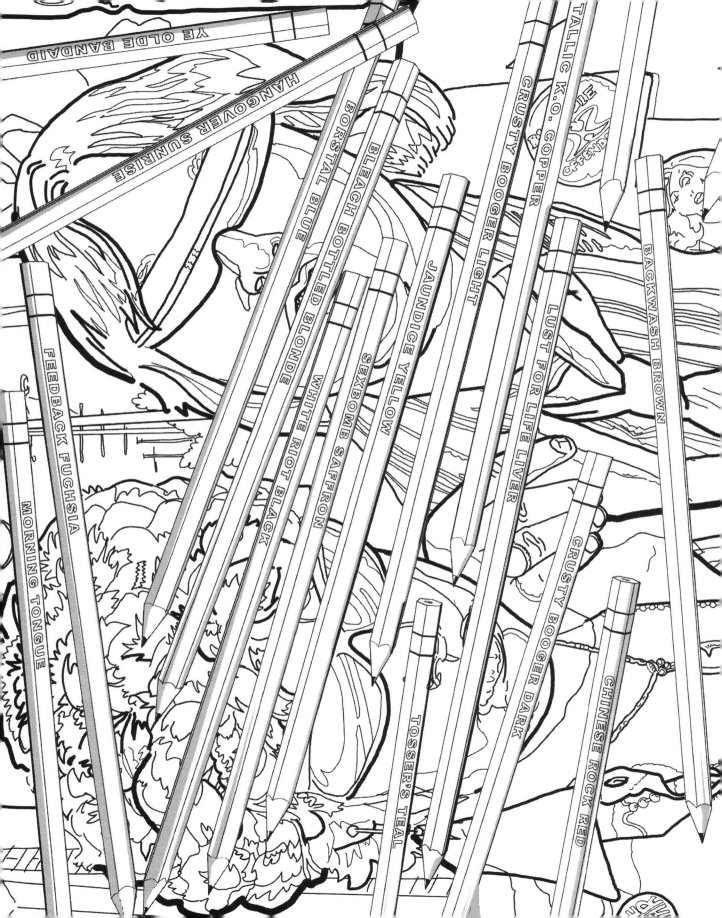

The source photo by Alex Levac was
taken of two punkish kids walking
on the Kings Road. I stuck the
On Broadway sign behind them in
order to include the scene in
San Francisco and furthermore to
signal that this is a coloring
book and not a history lesson.
Also, the thought that punk could
be represented by one person
leading a pal down the street by a
leash is kind of sweet.

Band Mates 1

This girl chopped the hair on one side of her head, added a few extra earrings and was punk as f**k.

I think that this girl was the
other one's friend. She's gone
and chopped off all of her hair and
added the studded dog collar in
case there was any question as to
how punk she was.

How much more "punk" can you get
than this guy? The spikey hair,
the leather jacket, the padlock
dangling from the belt loop, hell,
he's even drinking and smoking
in the bathroom. Jim Jocoy took
the source photo. He took lots
of pictures of punky people in
bathrooms and alleyways of late
70's LA.

This is a famous person but I'm
not going to say who it is.

Tear this page out and take it
to your barber or give it to a
drunk friend and indicate which
hairstyle you want.

This is Karen Ann Ooch from a
wierdo Jersey band called Steel
Tips. Why would anyone bother to
learn to the play the guitar if
you could look as cool as she does
just holding one?

When is a toilet not a toilet?

I took a few images from the movie
Rude Boy which is a movie that I
kind of hate.

This is from a short publication
"How to Look Punk" that covered
all of the steps it took to
remake your Debbie Boone loving
self into a genuine punk. The
author, Marliz, was billed as
"internationally known in the
industry for her ability in
current trend perception".

MAKE-UP LIKE A PUNK

...ant to look ... However, ...e eyes", a ...make-up. ...aquillage of ...nk rockers is ...the ocean. In ...the make-up ...nted on like a ...ns to be just ...ough looking. ...nise. It's a fun ...st "paint it on ...e the pogo all

...s a touch of the ...e of the quietly ...yes are heavily ...lower, with liner ...totally shadowed ...wo colors of eye ...e over-all design ...t at outer corners, ...ly dropped

Mascara is not important for the extremist pun... because it tends to distract from the studied ey... ...low designs. Blusher IS, however. Two shades ... ...t on the cheekbone and a dee... ...her as fac...

I took the super famous photo
taken by Janette Beckman of
Chet and Joe Okonkwo, a.k.a, the
"Islington Twins" and contrasted
their pork-pie hats and buttoned
up ace mod style against a sea
of bobbies in their custodian
helmets.

Homemade band fan t-shirt.

Once you start drawing electrical
cords, you just can't stop!

A dog collar, a chain, a punk
badge and a little spitting.

From a photo Kevin Cummins of
Manchester's Electric Circus.
Would everyone clear the stage so
that the roadie can break down the
gear!

Patchwork Union Jack.

British model and actress Jordan,
aka Pamela Rooke, in 1976. These
days she breeds Burmese cats.

When I finished putting together
all of the pages of this coloring
book I thought that I had only
included images that were taken
from 1976 through 1977. Then
I realized that this image of
slamming and moshing is clearly
from the 80's. I wish that I had
included an entry of fans pogoing
instead. So I don't get an A.

The subtlely applied punk details
challenge first impressions and
cause confusion.

Band Mates 2

Ice it first.

I added a couple of nods to
Vivienne Westwood to this group of
oddballs.

Members of The Cortinas serving
street attitude. From a Jill
Furmanovsky photograph.

From a source photo by Janette
Beckman, these girls were
attending a memorial for Sid
Vicious in Hyde Park.

The photographer Steve Johnston
said that he asked interesting
people that he saw on the Kings
Road if he could take their photo.
This leashed couple consented to
have their picture taken. He
said that he never heard from the
two models again. Have they ever
seen the photo? Did they buy a
copy of i-D magazine, tear out the
page with their photo and tape it
on the wall? Will they buy this
coloring book? Halfway through
coloring this page will the return
of long forgotten memories fill
them with meloncholy?

Jordan (again), Adam Ant (pre-
Prince Charming) and Gaye Advert
on a stage they never shared.

Radio Dogs

In Memorium

More products are available at
garyellisillustration.com or contact
noburbs@gmail.com

Printed in Great Britain
by Amazon